ON FAITH WE FLY

ON FAITH WE FLY

POETRY BY NATURE

KENNY LORD
A POET

authorHOUSE®

AuthorHouse™ LLC
1663 Liberty Drive
Bloomington, IN 47403
www.authorhouse.com
Phone: 1-800-839-8640

Published by AuthorHouse   08/16/2013

ISBN: 978-1-4918-1031-6 (sc)
ISBN: 978-1-4918-1032-3 (e)

Library of Congress Control Number: 2013915008

Contents

Preface

One important thing that I have found in life is that sometimes you have to dig deep down inside yourself and find the encouragement and drive, so as to put your best foot forward and accomplish the things that you want in life. We can't sit and wait for things to happen. They usually don't. I have always had a drive to try and accomplish things on my own. For me, that came from proper guidance when I was younger. From my grandparents, George and Olive Lord, who through many experiences in life, had the wisdom that I was blessed to be near and to receive. They were the best of the best. They taught me that the positive things that we do with our lives, can encourage others. I wanted to put this book together because I have a passion for poetry. A passion for different words that can be used to illustrate, to rhyme and to create. We all see life differently. No two individuals are the same and that has been my enjoyment. To read different versions of different ideas, put in many different ways. Also, to a tune within our minds, a sing song, a beat, a rhythm. Maybe, some humour mixed with something positive in someone's life and after reading this will get up and feel good about themselves and their family and friends. We owe it to ourselves in this timed life that we have, to be good with each other and feel good about every day that the sun rises. I really hope that you enjoy this book, that is from all different sides of my life; laughter, fiction, kindness, encouragement and love.

THIS BOOK IS DEDICATED TO THE TORONTO CHILDREN'S AID SOCIETY.

THANK YOU.

KENNY LORD (MILLER)—FORMER CROWN WARD.

A Cobbler Am I

Good day sir for a farthing I will,
I will fix your shoes for a smile and a thrill,
You will dance in the stars by the light of the moon,
And ill fix your shoes, while I whistle a tune,
Bring all that you can I will make you a pair
While the children watch while I sew,
They will smile as I tap with a hammer, then glue
I'm a coblers son you should know,
I cut the leather with a very sharp knife
And these shoes are the best in the land,
As i carefully cut and size just for you
With my knife and hammer and hand,
So I'm a cobbler yes, on a very good day
I can make you shoes for a dime,
Whether dancing shoes, or whatever you chose
I can make in a very short time.

All Seasons

I see the evergreens
On the prairies
Stunning, in green attire
Through cold, as if desire
On the highest mountains you stand free
Your smell is as fresh as a spring
And you dawn coloured lights that sing
Prickly pine, forever in time
Quiet on a hill, flowing still
In the wind, the evergreen blows a long soft hush
Then strong and whistles in chorus,
Rolling with the hills
Singing tunes of freedom
As they march in line,
Magically, blue spruce,

Of the ocean and sky, your blue ignites
Lasting sights
Deep green mighty
Christmas lights
Your season has no preference,
As you rest
Always green
Pure and clean
Winter garden of images wrapped in snow
But through the wind and warmth she reveals
And hearts with smiles is all she steals.

Always A Penguin

A friendly little fella wiggling by
With flippers and very wide feet,
A round black head with a dark little eye
In a black and white suit so neat,
Off in the water for a very cold swim
And some fish that are oh so yummy,
Swimming through the water then onto the ice
Where he slips right onto his tummy,
He talks with his friends who are all standing by
In sunny but very cold weather,
How I wish I could shop at all the nice stores
But I've been wearing these clothes forever

Angels That Fly

As we look out at the mountains
Our faith keeps us strong,
Our journey is gated by time
And our thoughts are long,
The pictures of each passing moment
Bring our eyes in search, to above
But our privilege to pass this way
Comes from a much greater love.

As I Grow Old

The daze of years, the shake of fears
I race towards the open skies,
I smile, for I did find my loves of life,
I had my strife, but carry on my heart the will,
In quiet search I ride the waves, no matter how
With courage I did always brave
To gather all the love, I save
Even though I never knew the wrath of time.
I cried, as one by one and blow by blow
I searched for you, till I did know,
Yet still, to live the ways I can
Means to live in peace, with me the man.

Banana Walk

Through the sugar cane fields of Rhodens I walk
Out into the many soft paths, of banana fields
The sun is beating down through many yields,
The hush with long wide leaves that fan
Some donkey rope and yellow yam,
The workers sing the island songs
Of toils but seem to find the laughter,
Canals refresh as cattle graze,
While John Crowe flies and seeks the after,
Tobacco huts send their amaze
The over proof, a quench of thirst
As a cutlass rests along the side,
Silence gently halts, as rose apples burst
The work begins again in stride,
Cool island breeze, banana trees
The island songs forever tell,
You are my calypso lady
Forever smile, I wish you well.

Barra Still

I taste the salty spray from dock
The Barra still, could beat the clock,
He wonders me as I stand brave
And feel the eager sun,
For he was there, as we did stare
Another gone for fun,
So where are you my king of speed?
I'm looking from the dock,
The glare proclaims a fighting chance
To see a star, a rock,
Oh there you are, you choose for me
To see you at your will,
You slice the water like a knife
The disappear, you thrill.

Before I Sleep, I Pray

Lord, thank you for each day of light
For every season and for the flowers that bloom,
Thank you for the dull days that turn to bright
And for the stars and sun and moon,
Thank you for my power to forgive
For the courage to help those in need,
For humanity as we strive to live
To own to love and cast out greed,
Thank you for the love of my family and friends
And help me to always appreciate each day of health,
Thank you for my starts and ends
And thank you for the poor and wealth,
Another journey has seen me by
The test of time has made me strong,
Compassion, humility and thankful till I die
No matter how short the day, or be it long,
I am truly blessed, I thank you god
Though the mountains get higher and steeper,
And help me to always remember in love
That I am my brother's keeper.

Boots

Today I walked a mile for you
In the boots I gave a shine,
I'll walk the trails, till good prevails
Till death sounds at the chime,
And when I walk through danger and
I stop to feel the air,
No fear inside, I got my ride
My boots will take me there,
Up to the doors, the stairs and floors
I'll pound the path of good,
The comfort of my boots is just
So little understood,
And so my boots, they keep me safe
There with me to the end,
They lay my path, they sooth my soul
They really are my friend,
So if I should die along the way
Protecting my sister and brother,
Take what you will, take everything
But my boots are for my mother.

Butterflies To Freedom

Soft wings make angels off to heaven
I wish for just a ride,
Though I am weak, I will be sure
To float gently by your side,
And fluttering I hear your path
The mist of colours, gardens grow
The children speak in their young hearts
Come fly with me, for this I know,
I'm floating out to space with you
I'm holding tight as eagles do,
For this I know that was is true
Is butterflies are free to fly.

Carousel

Musical box playing, as the carousel goes round and round
Galloping horses, with children riding, smile,
Holding poles, for young and olds
Laughing playgrounds, for just a longer while,
A journey to an away fantasy place in their dreams
Or so it seems, by what's at play,
Loved ones holding tight, much to their delight
Oh please daddy, please can I stay,
Slow rolling motions, waves like oceans
Toward a never before seen, their own land,
Just a bit faster, while the wind blows
But please daddy, hold onto my hand,
I know we will be there in just a while

As we circle, we drift out there,
I see it, a circus, playgrounds of colours
I won't leave my horse, I won't dare,
Up and down the horses glide
I cling to every thought,
Every second writes a new story
This fun just can't be taught,
It's getting slower, the horses stop
The circles lull, it may seem
But thoughts are hanging in their minds
Of this travelling musical dream

Cattle Drive From Buzzard Canyon

I was the lead hand on this cattle drive, from a small town in Pasadena
called dollar city.
We saddled up and rode hard throughout the night
Trailblazing past Snake River,
A few coyotes and some tombstones
Young hands with a slight shiver,
Longhorns were hold up in buzzard canyon
Rustlers probably in the brush where small fire burning,
Pistol packing with my Winchester
In behind, now cattles turning,
The mountains by Pasadena were the quickest way back to join the cattle
drive
So we hightailed it up the mountains, out onto the other side,
Through Indian Territory, buffalo grazing
A few coyotes, was a tough ride,
Fifty head of cattle and all were branded
Had to lasso a young calf, only a young stray,
Be back with the main drive
By the start of the day,

Along bison river we stopped to water
We unsaddled the horses for a spell,
Before the crack of dawn we arrived with the drive
Looked at the cattle boss, nodded, all is well,
So we headed back to dollar city along stagecoach trail
Reached it finally, by high noon,
What a man wouldn't do for some wieners and beans
A long bath and a drink at the saloon,
The marshal was told of where the bushwhackers were hold up
And he got a possee and headed with some high rolling shooters,
Finally caught them just past buzzard canyon
They were known rustlers and looters,
By now i had some good grub, fancy duds and apple pie
Got paid and pondered settling down in town for a while,
A good cigar, seeing padre at the church up yonder
Greeting the senioritas with a word and a smile,
So I bought a ranch just outside of town
Peaceful, some cattle, horses, don't hear any hollars,
My seniorita and I watch the sun rise and sunset
The good lord on my mind and a few silver dollars.

Circus Show

Step right up and see the show
With horses around the ring,
For just a small admission see
A monkey try to sing,
Popcorn, candy, elephants too
That stand up in the air,
Tightrope walkers, trapeze artist
And tigers in a pair,
Costumes that are made of glitter
A ringmaster centre stage,
A fire breather, dancing clowns
Who never act their age,
A magic show, pipe organs blow
The music's all around,
Come see the funny mimes that move
And never make a sound,
The human cannonball that blasts
A man into a net,
The biggest tent you've ever seen
So no one's getting wet,
Come one and all and bring your friends
You'll get your monies worth,
Come see the circus, that's in town
The greatest show on earth.

Cookies For Santa

Before I go to bed at night
And wait for Christmas day,
I will leave some cookies out for him
When he drives up on his sleigh,
He rides through the night, at the speed of light
As he travels around the world,
He's a tired old man with a big bag of toys
And his white beards always curled,
Stop for a cookie and a glass of milk
And rest for a while on my couch,
And take off your boots and your big red hat
And you're Christmas list and your pouch,
The journey is tough as you travel so far
And Rudolph is lighting your way,
But time for a cookie will make you strong
As you get ready for Christmas day,
So ride again, in the snow or the rain
That nice little snack was so yummy,
Jingle bells as reindeers fly
Now my belt is too tight for my tummy

Cuckoo Clock

I hear your tick, I hear your tock
Your wooden house does hide,
As minutes and the hours go
You're out for one more ride,
You're such a clever cuckoo bird
Whose sound does crave attention,
Out from your little house you show
And cuckoo your invention,
Your intricate, such craftsmanship
Portrays a work of art,
A pretty bird, but same old word
As out the house you dart,
You're made for kings, you're made for queens
You're made for one and all,
This little bird, word after word
Is hung from every wall,
When night is here and children dear
They rest their little head,
You must be quiet, stay inside
It's time to go to bed.

Drop By Drop

The last time it rained
I wondered when
Those tiny droplets
Would soon become a puddle,
So that I could walk upon
What used to be a cloud.

Fairytales And Gumballs

I gaze at rolling twists and twirls
The bells are sounding pillars of light,
Through rosy eyes I see my own
My fairytales and gumballs glee,
My chant of smile and I see the rainbows
Rolling, bouncing, red and green
I love you gold, my beauty queen,
As age is sure, I see the wand
Of sparkling stars and brews of wishes
I cling with hope as she still goes
Around the bends all lined with silver,
For once upon a time I see
The beauty in the quest for love,
The happy ever after eyes that close
The many bubbles of my morning greets
As soon she rolls and takes no seats,
And only for a moment slows
In lands so far with scent of raz,
And maybe fruits of gardens bed,
And then the damsel soon is safe
And god has answered one more dream,
As I watch the ball that moves like stream,
The journey nears its final rest
As I am in awe of a place called peace.

Fall

Autumn leaves, cool morning breeze
A taste of chill, the blowing trees,
And evergreen, my passion still
Will light my evening star,
No need to justify your pure
Your answer high, so far
I wait for you, I scent your call
Sure to the time, I figure fall,
Behind the wall, I see the red
Of Christmas ribbons and the sled,
The old man waits his turn to ride,
And make the children smile and hide,
I gleam your time, I see the way
Another smile true to your day,
I'll grab my tackle and my rod
And thank you for your beauty god,
For I see your grey
I hear your gaul,
I feel content
It must be fall.

Frog On A Lily

Proudly you stand and throw your chest
In the pond on floating lily,
You catch the insects one by one,
You really look so silly,
I see you look at me so still
With small but bulging eyes,
And there you go, a leaping hop
Big jump for such a size,
Your skin so slippery to the feel
You would be hard to catch,
And as for that big round tummy
That's very hard to match,
I really think we could be friends
Like me and groundhog willy,
I'll hold you soft and feed you lots
If you just get off that lily.

Gentle Stream

From the mountain comes a clear cool stream that floats continuous
time toward the open river.
So pure and determined.
It runs over the mossy rocks that line the waters edge and provides
comfort.
I hear the deep bubbly drop of wash going by, as it waves in sways and
seems to dance.
Some trickles at the side of the stream appear to branch off toward
another home.
Imagination joins branches and bits of straw going bye.
Cheerfully, a tiny petal swims.
Sometimes, a little fish fights to join the wet journey.
Slowly, I breath in the fresh draft of the moving past, refreshing life
along the way, i seem to loose my thoughts for fields.
The sun reflects on the streams depth and shows a clear view.
The stream will stay till seasons change
But I will not alter my right of you

Good Morning Mr Clown

Can you make me laugh like you did before
Can you make me a little cat,
Can I please have a big balloon
As you smile and wear your funny hat,
Will you sit with me, will you stay a while
So I can tell all my friends,
Will you sing a song and dance with me
So the music never ends,
You're full of colours, with a big red nose
And your shoes are oh so funny,
Your clothes are all colours of the rainbow
You look so bright and sunny,
Lollipops and candy sticks
You really are a winner,
But my mom says I have to wait
Until I have had my dinner,
So promise me when I awake
And from my window comes a glare,
I will have the biggest smile again
For you will still be here.

Harbour Lights

On the boat adrift in the harbour. I stare at the dark shoreline stage, with
open curtains that introduce the neon lights of a city at rest.
Peacefully, I mark each coloured building with my eyes, that are
suspended in amazement. Reading all of the flashing signs, the calm of
the lake, with buoys and more marking channel lights, seem to meet the
introduction of archetectual beauty.
I wonder.
Who has seen the other side of the mountain? Who quests, while others
sleep?
Seagulls fascinate on the water and follow my roll, as if to question.
I know your there too, freedom fish.
my rocking boat is a counting tune, cradled by a soft and smiling moon.
Coloured reflections spread across the calm lake, thrown from the land
that breathes.
I smell the lake breeze and the bright evening star points pure and true.
Other captains do the same, I'm sure,
Other fishermen content, with line and lure,
The silence seems to sail the globe of worldly seamen, one after one.
I can hear morgans thoughts.
The lights of leisure entice land,
But I will watch from the waters hand.

Humming Bird

Rippling twitter, hums so soft
Over bridge and over loft,
You gently take your share in beek
As you go your hide and seek,
Your colours might,
Your tail extend,
A standout in the flowers blend,
I stare and gaze as interest rise
You took the charm, you took the prize,
And when I wake from such a dream,
I'll look again for such serene.

Jack The Bear

Hold me tight when you need a friend
When you're scared or feeling sad,
I am very soft and very warm
And I never, ever get mad,
You can tickle my tummy to make me laugh
I will always smile right back,
I will remember your name, please do the same
I go by the name of jack,
I can dance for you if you close your eyes
You will see me move my feet,
I can sing like a bird and carry a tune
And my clothes are always so neat,
If you cry I will hear you and always be near you
So hold me close to your heart,
I will speak to you softly, just to let you know
I am there at the end or the start,
My eyes are so big but happy they are
And I see you all through the day,
So hold my hand while I walk with you
While we jump and skip as we play,
I'm a little brown bear with thick bushy hair
And I came from a very special pack,
If you hug me tight, you will be alright
And I go by the name of jack

Joey Harmonica

His name was Joey harmonica.
Old but jazz, he could make the right hum
He could gather your thoughts out west,
He could move with the breeze, over mountains and trees
Make a tune is what he did best,
He warmed the hearts of the lonely loves
And would bring a young man to a tear,
He played with the moon and sometimes a spoon
A tap from his foot or a pair,
A bright evening star that shines from afar
And wolves that came out to howl,
And Joey would play by evening or day
By the tick of the clock or an owl,
It was fifty five when Joey died
And the sounds of the night came to rest,
Make horses lay down and take away frown
That's Joey, that's what he did best.

Jude The Obscure

In the priceless beauty of Nova Scotia, we found you,
And you were to forever be sketched in our hearts,
As ours.
The behold of a new treasure of the earth to us.
For we are in love and you are one of the bonds of beauty, that gathers
our journey of sacred, along the paths to always.
So be it.
So be your timely scent of slight fruit, so different.
So be the excellence of nature, true to god.
So be Jude, to be as she pleases and teases.
So be the smile that is sent with her view.
So be a secret of the absolute charms of life.
So be the creations of the shines of petals so true.
So be the gift of you, that we give to ones we love.
So be your colours in gardens of grace.
So be our rose, Jude the obscure.

Little Man

If I could walk among the grass
And be the height of blade,
With paper pieces, bits of glass
And chewing gum that someone made,
Some soft grass and pointy weeds
Big ants in living mounds,
Slightly damp with little seeds
Live thick among the grounds,
Sprinkler heads, some garden beds
Beware of fields of play,
Where children run and parks are green
Could be my last of day,
The roots of trees, safe from the breeze
Is all the earth will give,
It really takes the outdoor ones
To find a place to live

Little White Church

Up on a hill, just a very short walk
Through evergreen trees and birch,
A bridge over stream that trickles by
There's a path to a little white church,
A steeple up top with a cross below
And stained glass to make you smile,
With mahogany pews and hanging lights
Come in and pray for a while,
As small as a room that you go to sleep
With an alter of candles and brass,
The sunlight rays that shine right through
And kneel as time does pass,
It's where I go in my mind sometimes,
Where my pain and troubles cease,
This little white church on a hill up yonder
Where I go to find my peace.

Lucky Lady

Standing in the garden and what do I see
A ladybug decided to land on me,
Three wishes, china dishes, dreams that come true
Ice cream and roses, all will be free,
She floated so slowly and softly touched down
I smiled at her costume of dots,
A round little shell with a very small head
She jumped right on me from the pots,
Who can I tell of my fate full of luck
As my lady walks over my skin,
A brand new car or a house full of gold
And surely a lottery win,
I think with a smile, for she is my luck
As I stand on the grass, not the worst,
So off mister bee and off mister wasp
For the lady is always first.

Magicland

Candy sticks that swirl so high
Reflect like diamonds, stare in awe
I fly so high to meet the clouds
The sun so close as ice does thaw,
What height is where the dreams come true
And love remains for me and you,
As if to bring the brightest star
The sparkle bright in night of tar,
Oh speak to me my love of chant
Forever in your heart, god grant,
I softly float in realms so light
Delight me, for the time is right,
When I awake it's you I see
The smile that fuses love,
Forvever in our hearts will be
Until we meet above

My Grandmothers Parrot

This poem was written when I was 9 years old. It was the first poem I ever remember writing and I have always kept it.

"my grandmother had a parrot
Whos colours were like a carrot,
When she gave it away, I cried and I prayed
I wanted my grandmothers parrot".

This parrot was donated to the Hope Gardens zoo, in Kingston, Jamaica, where it lived happily ever after.

Peace Till Twilight

I see you close your eyes my child
As I gently rock you still,
You lay so softly as you smile
And close your eyes at will,
Though you see me not, I smile right back
A tear rolls down my face,
So thankful for your gift of life
I love you god of grace,
I know you dream of clowns that dance
And fill your eyes with laughter,
So soft and gentle, heart of gold
I'll love you, even after,
And when you awake, I'll still be here
As you come from by and by,
first thing you see, it will be me
With a smile and wink of an eye

Peter Popsicle

Please wait for a minute mister popsicle man
For I'm running to my dad just as fast as I can,
I can hear your bell as you ring down the road
I can see your box with the popsicle load,
I'm getting some money for a popsicle treat
I cleaned my room and it really looks neat,
He has blue ones and green ones and orange ones too
Daddy please can I have some money from you,
So off to the cart I rush out the house
I'm happy and so very glad,
Can I have a popsicle, an orange one please
Make it two cause ones for my dad.

Playground Laughters

Childrens laughter, filled with glee
A funny scream as down the slide,
I see them not for they are far
The echoes speed, ride after ride,
Little voices with covered hats
They dream of puppies, rabbits and cats,
Another swing, another song
Their laughter pure, their jumps are long,
More yells and screams, I smile with them
More playing in the sand,
And driving boats and giving jokes
She has a magic wand,
Soon through the sprinkler, soaking wet
The sand is gone for now,
It's getting cold, a towel hugs
My eyes and cheeks and brow,
It's time to go, the clock moves on
To home without a peep,
They rub their eyes as quiet shares
And soon their off to sleep

Progressive Relaxations—Falling Drop

I look up at the dark green leaf that holds that soft drop it slowly looks over the edge of the leaf, pleading for a way to escape natures grasp. The sun peers through the edge of time, chanting for this gift to fall. The crystal clear reflection of moving colours are all that signals movement. The tear like drop crawls quietly over the slippery wax like surface of open face. For a brief moment it stops. Then, a gentle blowing wind starts a whole new journey again and again. In full view now, I learn of the beauty of water. Now, it is time, as she crawls toward the edge and finally, cautiously, the water drop is now in the hands of gravity. Through the air, floating, with changing shapes, of natures pure, guided toward earths floor. The earth smiles as it waits to catch the wet crystal quench. My eyes focused, I watch. As still as I could hope, I smile and wait for the soft push among the green blades of grass. I hear the crickets speak and the birds chirp. For it has found its resting place among the fields and I will sleep away the morning dew.

Progressive Relaxation—Port Royal

Along the dock, I sit. My drifting mind is toward a seagull that flies and moves with the sea breeze. I wonder who is free to fly at will, like you. I smile. Your sound, with sailing ships does sooth the mind to travel through peaceful realms, while sand does quietly watch and glare through eternal rays of sun. Small boats move with still, quiet people, who face the wind with peace and ease. In the distance at shore, parade grounds breathe and await the return of the heroes that keep our safe. Maybe one day, I will be able to walk the ocean floor and really see many magical ocean secrets. A star fish proclaims the path, a fish pot that collects my thoughts, many treasures of man, hidden for years and saved by the cold, callus, depths. Look, there's a sting ray, swaying from side to side and rolling with a tide and another tide. An old Spanish Galleon where I see the hull that holds many secrets of its doom. I think, as I see a buoy, very old on the water, a pelican's bench, where he watches for his next meal. Oh, that salty smell with sea weed, delivering much needed peace to my body. The mangroves are funny. They choose to plant the ocean floor as they slowly laugh in the same sweet wind that puts my mind on that raft that has untied and is now afloat at the harbour mouth. What will happen to it? When will it cease. Will it float for a while and give colourful dolphin some shade, outwards by the banks. Deep in thought I rest, with again that seagull call, that continues with very short breaks. And I hear you too; you fried fish smell that comes from shore behind me. Then, with a tease in the breeze, you are gone. Time slows in the harbour. The breeze seems to push back time and hold it gently. I am week in the eyes at the calm waters that are like a soft lullaby, that whispers. As the dock warms my hands and feet, I begin to count the weeds as they float by, forever you roll out of the harbour, toward the open sea. And I will float always in my countless dreams, of Port Royal Harbour, with a soft splash, bubbly blue deep and warm lines through the hush air of forever out to sea.

Sailors Voyage

Farewell my love, my ship sets sail
To brave the seas of chance,
But you will see me, in your heart
While out to sea you glance,
The waves that roll the oceans deep
And take me far alone,
Will steer my course through stormy seas
But also bring me home,
And when I'm at sea, I will sing a song
As the sun sets on the blue,
I see you smile along the pier
When I sail back to you.

Seaside

When I lay back in my fishing chair
I breathe in the gusts of sea breeze,
The rolling waves bring peaceful messages,
Marlins dance, sailfish swim
Dolphins delight the spectacle of the eye,
Until I die, I will live a fisherman.
The hoot of the whale, a time to sail
The slow wash of water weeds at peace.
And sometimes out of pure interest
The little ones do swim up top
And throw a bubble drop by drop,
They show there here as well.
When waves do slow and sun will glow
Will show the waters deep,
I see the sunfish and the star
The Barra, just a peep,
And oh they fly by waters edge
They float from wave to wave,
And deep below, a wreck of time
Now just the oceans grave,
Soon comes the setting of the sun
A marvel to end the day,
Won't miss the waters of the night
I'll wait just one more day.

Soldiers Footsteps

Away from home and across the seas
They fight for our freedom still,
Over dark lands and distant voices
With silence and strong will,
Sometimes beyond their sense of things
They battle with every breath,
But we honour our heroes protecting us
In life and sometimes death,
And one by one, courageously
They face the unknown fears,
They fight for peace in lands back home
In pain and fighting tears,
God keep them safe and bring them home
As they walk the fields at war,
We will pray until we hear
Their footsteps at our door.

Smile with me Kristi

When I am gone and you miss my love
I am always watching you from up above,
Remember kindness I showed to you
Remember always, love is true,
Be courageous through the rough water
And never forget that you are my daughter,
When you have those days, that you just want to cry
I will be right in your heart, just look at the sky,
So be at peace always, my angel, my guide
I will be waiting in heaven, with arms open wide.

Still We Dance

I smiled for you and took my steps
And saw the music through,
I watched you smile, so proud of us
Twas only you who knew
All through our hearts, we swayed in hope
We knew that you were proud,
A little twist, a little glide
I'll keep her safe, I vowed,
She's just like you, so beautiful
The elegant look you show,
She smiles so bright, a beaming sight
A gift of love I know
I watch her as she sparkles bright,
This day is hers and so too night,
I hold her softly to a tune,
As we both stare at eyes of moon,
I cradle her in arms of steel

Her stunning smile, such strong appeal,
As if in flight, I float in peace
And watch you smile, so mild,
You have that right to be amazed
For she is all your child,
Now you are gone, but I still dance
If even in my heart,
I try to have that step again
Can't recreate the art,
I keep her warm, I keep her safe,
She's always in my glance,
We miss you mom, please smile with us
Keep watching as we dance

Sweet Kayla

From the time you were born, of Love and strength
You gave us smiles of forever time,
Our hope was always there with you
From you we see that Love is true,
Surrounding you with hands that hold
You're every move so you are safe,
When God above does grant more time
He lets you teach us, line by line,
The way that children learn to Love
Comes from the father, up above,
So when the time does come to be
We must practise what you taught,
Eternal close beside you be
Then close our eyes, forget you not,
Forever in our hearts you walk.

The Drummer Played On

Drum, drum, here we come
Over boom, explosive fields,
Tears of nitro,
Cheeks of fire,
The drummer played on.
Many died that day,
As over the fields they lay,
In silence.
The drum was taken back
And placed beside a Union Jack.

The Old Pin Stripe

The red pin stripe has found its way
Up another blue path of gloom,
A young man fights to hear himself
Lest he falls to silent doom,
We cannot fail, although we try
To pry our image deep,
And daisys will not cover us
Too soon for lasting sleep,
A piper is that tune that we
Shall cherish as we go,
For music calms the roughest seas
And sets our hearts aglow,
Our strength within, our loved ones see
Remain our burn desire,
Is that of who we work beside
And sets the drive on fire,

Through autumn leaves and winter chills
We walk that path of right,
No shift is over, true to god
Till all are home at night,
And every home on every street
Shall sleep because we dare,
To keep the watch in every land
No matter what the scare,
And when this day is over
And my maker I will sight,
I will say for all that died for cause
I love that old pin stripe.

The Pond At Rhodens

Where I loved to think.
The peaceful site of turtles cove
Or where I would go to make a wish,
Sometimes my horse would eat the grass
And stand by me with pond like glass,
I had that place, still, so gracefully
Mother, I think of you often.
A coconut drops to break silence, as if to speak
Hibiscus and green parakeet,
Green lizard guards from the tamarind tree.
One seldom sees the thoughts of breeze
That lay to rest upon us.
The fish fry from old harbour square
Glides like surf and cuts the air,
In the distance I see the melon fields
Where I would cool to the earth,
Mongoose goes by, maybe dragon fly,
Soon, the pond would seem to listen
With such soft pace,
Truthful.
To fulfil more passing time,
I returned to her,
And reached out to another friend of the island songs.

Tide

Softly and quietly, the foamy waves roll
Toward the sparkling soft sand
Peacefully they sway the magic wand,
I hear the foam in seaside breeze
The hollow sound just seems to please,
The guiding drift is true and clean
I smile to you my loving friend
That gentle you that has no end,
And very slowly you gather your mist
Of drip and wet and stand the pace of time.
Again and again, like peaceful rain
You explore your bounty,
While giving thanks it seems
You pray for another,
Unlike no other, you roll again your true thoughts,
And I, I am still there,
I feel your calm as it wets me so
In warm surrender, sooths my soul,
Oh lady peace, as you roll another wave
And hush, so still, to sea i gaze,
You will not halt till time do cease
I love you so, eternal peace.

Towards Victory

I will go into this fight with an armour of steel
And with the heart of my being,
I will refuse defeat and pursue victory.
Though the day seems to desire not
I will not lose my sight of pride
My character and integrity will bloom through time
And with the strength of my greatest will
I will find that last ounce of courage
And stand proud at the finish,
True to self and true to god.

Walk Good My Child

There will be times when you will laugh
And times when you will cry,
For there is a time for us to live
And a time for us to die,
A time for Christmas and Easter too
When you're walking down the isle,
So proud of you, you look amazing
Just watch me as I smile,
Times can be tough and journeys rough
Remember love is true,
Be kind to all and never fall
For skies are always blue,
Be polite, it's always right
And make sure you're on time,
Face the world and feel proud
Trust me you'll be fine,
Never give up, is how we live
Face every task at hand,
For it is better to live with ourselves
Then stepped on in the sand,
I will come to you within your heart
When you look up towards a star,
I will always be with you as you walk
I promise, I won't be far.

Walking Proud

I took my first steps when I walked with you
I have walked in the early morning dew,
I walked at night when I was so afraid
And walked at school where friends were made,
I walked for charity that was close to my heart
I walked at the beach with sunsets of art,
I walked through the pages of books in my head
And I walked through the dreams of my children in bed,
I walked to my love on the day that we met
A walk full of happiness, I will never forget,
I walk every hour of grace in a day
And I walk to my knees, when I am to pray,
I walk for others so they can rest
And I walk for the hope when they do their best,
But when I am most proud, with the things I choose
Is when I walk in someone else's shoes.

Watermelon Seeds

Don't eat the seeds my grandpa said
There not like eating a pear,
Watermelon seeds if swallowed they will
Start growing right out of your ear,
Black slippery seeds that grow so quick
Are best to cast aside,
Just eat the red, much sweeter instead
And watch for seeds that glide,
And if you happen to swallow a seed today
You thought, but really don't know,
Make sure in the morning to check your ears
To see if a melon did grow.

When You Return

My husband,
I will be here when you return,
I will hear the battle cries when you fight for our freedom and hear
chariots roll,
I will feel the sword that maybe wounds your skin, but not the soul,
Not even through clashes and brave ones falling
Could ever, no never, keep us apart,
The sounds of clashing armour will be my hope.
For your heart has made you mighty.
But my love, when in the battle, take not your mind from task at hand,
Take not your eyes off any man,
I know you well, brave soul, proud knight,
Back down you won't, from any fight,
And as wounded, scared, but breathing still,
Coming home to me remains my will,
And when you return and see my light,
You will know my love shines bright
For loyal I will always be
Come home my love, come home to me.

Write To Her

Could I,
For fear of sorrow, even then tomorrow
For what had been, something maybe seen,
But for you my path was paved with chances bright
I still loved you with all my might,
So I will be still, not in the den
So seeing you could be again,
The blame has past as age becomes
I cannot put to paper, for I
Should love you till the day I die,
my mother, whom I never knew
We walked together, two by two
Such eyes of might, yet soft with fright
I knew you and only you
For twice with you I caught your eyes
Our hearts are joined as one,
So not to write is no surprise
For I am still your son

Young Bear

I hear the words so strong in grief
As you take the front of pain,
You choke back tears, of 15 years
Your eyes conceal, no shame,
Yes he is gone my father friend
I'll show him what he's taught,
The courage he instilled in us
I listened and I caught,
I promised her we will be ok
As I touched my little man,
The toils of life, the unknown strife
We will do this, yes we can,
I think ahead as I console
The hurt it's like no other,
My father's gone, I will stand strong
For my mother and my brother

To My Wife Tisha

"WE SHARE A JOURNEY OF LOVE THAT'S TRUE

YOU ARE MY LOVE AND YOU ARE MY FRIEND,

THANK YOU FOR OUR LIFE THAT'S JOINED

ON FAITH WE FLY, FOR US, THERE IS NO END.".

I UNDERSTAND MARIA
AND I LOVE YOU.

Your Son;

Kenny

About the Author

Kenneth Keith (Kenny) Lord (Miller) was born in Toronto, Canada, to a very young teenager and at two years of age, became a Crown Ward of the Toronto Children's Aid Society. After being in their care and Foster homes for a few years, he went through the International Adoption process and was adopted to a Jamaican family and went to live in Kingston, Jamaica. For many years, Kenny was raised by his adopted grandparents and was fortunate enough to be educated at the prestigious boy's Private boarding school, DeCarteret College, in Mandeville, which is in the centre of the Island. At 17 years of age, he returned to Canada to further his education and to find his biological parents.

Kenny attended London South Secondary school in London, Ontario and graduated with his high school diploma. He then attended George Brown College in Toronto where he took the three year Watchmaking program. Immediately after College, he was hired by Birks Jewellers in Toronto as a Watchmaker. About two years later, Kenny had a change of heart and began a career in the Security field that would last a few years. He went back to College and graduated from Seneca College in the Police Science programme. Eventually, Kenny was fortunate enough to be hired by the Toronto Police Service as a Cadet, graduating from the Ontario Police College and the Toronto Police College and was then sworn in as a Police Constable, where he is now in his 25ᵗʰ year. He is married and is the father of three adult children. He lives in Whitby, Ontario, which is a part of the Greater Toronto Area.

Three of the Poems in this book, were written when Kenny was living in Jamaica, as a young teenager, while attending DeCarteret College. Throughout the years, he has written poetry as a hobby and has kept most of them. This book is a collection of poetry throughout the years that he has decided to publish in a book for your enjoyment.